PRAYERS

■ OUT OF THE ■

DEPTHS

Healing Words for Times
of Depression

LTP

LITURGY
TRAINING
PUBLICATIONS

ACKNOWLEDGMENTS

We are grateful to the many publishers and authors who have given permission to include their work. Every effort has been made to determine the ownership of all texts and to make proper arrangements for their use. We will gladly correct in future editions any oversight or error that is brought to our attention.

Unless otherwise noted, excerpts from scripture are from the *New American Bible with Revised New Testament and Psalms*, copyright © 1991, 1986, 1970 Confraterniy of Christian Doctrine, Inc., Washington, D.C. Used with permission. All rights reserved. No portion of the *New American Bible* may be reprinted without permission in writing from the copyright holder.

Excerpts from scripture on pp. 2, 16, 17, 29, 31, 34, 47, 51, and 54 are from the *New Revised Standard Version* of the Bible © 1989, Division of Christian Education of the National Council of the Churches of Christ in the United States of America. Used by permission. All rights reserved.

Acknowledgments continued on page 56.

PRAYERS OUT OF THE DEPTHS © 2003 Archdiocese of Chicago: Liturgy Training Publications, 1800 North Hermitage Avenue, Chicago IL 60622-1101; 1-800-933-1800, fax 1-800-933-7094, e-mail orders@ltp.org. All rights reserved. See our website at www.ltp.org.

This book was compiled by Mary Caswell Walsh and edited by Lorie Simmons with help from Laura Goodman. Carol Mycio was the production editor. The design is by Anna Manhart, who also did the typesetting in Galliard, Minion, and Trajan. Cover and interior art © 2002 Getty Images.

Printed in the United States of America.

Library of Congress Control Number: 2003106875

ISBN 1-56854-451-0

PDEPTH

CONTENTS

FOREWORD

Few illnesses are more painful, isolating, and exhausting than depression—for those who suffer from it and for their companions. Scripture calls it a sorrow gnawing at the human heart (Proverbs 25:20). It may be mild, brief, severe, or prolonged and may emerge for various reasons. Loss of a loved one or a traumatic experience may leave people depressed, or the illness may be triggered by a medical condition. Some people become depressed from negative ways of thinking or self-destructive ways of behaving learned early in life. Depression may also arise from chemical states in the body and sometimes a predisposition is inherited. Whatever the cause, depression brings suffering. Like all experiences, it has spiritual dimensions and prayer can help. "The LORD hears when I call out" (Psalm 4:4).

Prayer complements medical and psychotherapeutic treatments. It consoles those who grieve and restores an interior sense of safety to those who have been traumatized. Prayer offers strength and hope to cope with disabling illness. Prayer sustains us in our spiritual struggles; it helps us turn from negative thinking and self-destructive behaviors to healthy, holy, and life-giving thoughts and actions. Prayer leads us out of the isolation of depression into the healing power of communion, out of darkness into light and life. And prayer fortifies the companions of those struggling with depression, helping them cultivate balance and self care as they support their loved one.

Many holy people throughout history have suffered from depression and have contributed their wisdom to this little book. We can draw on their experiences, trusting that the God who sustained them in their darkness and lifted them into light will do the same for us. When the depression lifts and we are able to enjoy the beauty of creation and the wonder of our own lives, we give thanks. Gratitude supports and nurtures our new found health, opening our hearts to the fullness of God's love.

People experience depression in different ways at different times. Not all prayers and reflections in this book will be suitable for everyone or fitting for every moment. As you read, allow the Holy Spirit, our healer, companion, and consoler, to be your guide. And be confident that the God who loves us desires our healing.

—*Mary Caswell Walsh*

MY GOD,

MY GOD,

WHY HAVE YOU

ABANDONED

ME?

—PSALM 22:2

PRAYERS FOR HELP AND CONSOLATION

Out of the depths I call to you, LORD;
   Lord, hear my cry!
May your ears be attentive
   to my cry for mercy.

I wait with longing for the LORD,
   my soul waits for his word.
My soul looks for the Lord
   more than sentinels for daybreak.
More than sentinels for daybreak,
   let Israel look for the LORD.
For with the LORD is kindness,
   with him is full redemption.

—*Psalm 130:1–2, 5–7*

Ah Lord, my prayers are dead, my affections
dead, and my heart is dead: but thou art a
living God and I bear myself upon thee.

—*William Bridge, seventeenth century*

1

Like a slave who longs for the shadow,
   and like laborers who look for their wages,
so I am allotted months of emptiness,
   and nights of misery are apportioned to me.
When I lie down I say, "When shall I rise?"
   But the night is long,
   and I am full of tossing until dawn.

When I say, "My bed will comfort me
   my couch will ease my complaint,"
then you scare me with dreams
   and terrify me with visions,
so that I would choose strangling
   and death rather than this body.
I loathe my life; I would not live forever.
   Let me alone, for my days are a breath.
What are human beings, that you make
      so much of them,
   that you set your mind on them,
visit them every morning,
   test them every moment?
Will you not look away from me for a while?

—*Job 7:2–4, 13–19a*

In me there is darkness,
But with thee there is light,
I am lonely, but thou leavest me not.
I am feeble in heart, but thou leavest me not.
I am restless, but with thee there is peace.
In me there is bitterness, but with thee there
    is patience;
Thy ways are past understanding, but
Thou knowest the way for me.

—*Dietrich Bonhoeffer, twentieth century*

LORD, hear my prayer;
    let my cry come to you.

I am withered, dried up like grass,
    too wasted to eat my food.
From my loud groaning
    I become just skin and bones.
I am like a desert owl,
    like an owl among the ruins.
I lie awake and moan,
    like a lone sparrow on the roof.

I eat ashes like bread,
    mingle my drink with tears.

—*Psalm 102:2, 5–8, 10*

God, Father of Mercies, save me from the
hell within me. I acknowledge thee, I adore
and bless thee, whose throne is in heaven,
with thy Blessed Son and crucified Jesus,
and thy Holy Spirit.

—*Robert Leighton, seventeenth century*

My God, my God, why have you abandoned me?
Why so far from my call for help,
from my cries of anguish?
My God, I call by day, but you do not answer;
by night, but I have no relief.
Yet you are enthroned as the Holy One;
you are the glory of Israel.
In you our ancestors trusted;
they trusted and you rescued them.
To you they cried out and they escaped;
in you they trusted and were not disappointed.
But I am a worm, hardly human,
scorned by everyone, despised by the people.

Yet you drew me forth from the womb,
made me safe at my mother's breast.
Upon you I was thrust from the womb;
since birth you are my God.
Do not stay far from me,
for trouble is near,
and there is no one to help.

—Psalm 22:2–7, 10–12

No fire could warm this place
though the air hang in sultry shred and the
    roof perspire;
nothing here is amenable to fire.

Words fall in slow icy rain and freeze
upon the heart's sudden dismantled trees,
and branches break and fall.
From the wind of inclement glances I cannot
    shield myself
who find their frost too subtle to forestall
I am waiting for the snow of my own obscurity
    to settle
and cover me, frozen ground,
to blunt all sharp insufferable sound,
to meet the angles of cold and obliterate
    them all.

I long to rise in this room and say,
    "You are not my people,
I come from a warm country; my country is love.
Nor did I wish to come here: I was misdirected."
But their frost is not defied and their cold
    is not rejected.

So chilled am I by this presence of human winter
I cannot speak or move.

—*Jessica Powers (Sister Miriam, OCD), twentieth century*

How long, LORD? Will you utterly forget me?
  How long will you hide your face from me?
How long must I carry sorrow in my soul,
  grief in my heart day after day?

—*Psalm 13:1–3a*

O Holy Paraclete! sweetest consolation of the sorrowful! gracious Spirit! O come down with your mighty power into the deep recesses of our hearts! Lighten there with your brightness every dark retreat, enrich all with the dew of your abundant comfort! Kindle our inward parts with holy fervor, that the incense of our prayers and praises may always go up to you, O our God—through Jesus Christ, your Son, our Lord.

—*Saint Anselm of Canterbury, eleventh century*

Why are you downcast, my soul;
  why do you groan within me?
Wait for God, whom I shall praise again,
  my savior and my God.

I say to God, "My rock,
  why do you forget me?"
Why must I go about mourning
  with the enemy oppressing me?"

Why are you downcast, my soul;
  why do you groan within me?
Wait for God, whom I shall praise again,
  my savior and my God.

—*Psalm 42:6, 10, 12*

That prayer has great power
Which a person makes with all his might
It makes a sour heart sweet,
    A sad heart merry,
    A poor heart rich,
    A foolish heart wise,
    A timid heart brave,
    A sick heart well,
    A blind heart full of sight,
    A cold heart ardent.
It draws down the great God
    into the little heart,
It drives the hungry soul up
    into the fullness of God.
It brings together two lovers,
    God and the soul,
In a wondrous place where they speak
    much of love.

—*Mechthilde of Magdeburg, thirteenth century*

O God, you care for your creation with great tenderness. In the midst of overwhelming pain, you offer hope. Give help to me, whose spirit seems to be lost and whose soul is in despair. Let me feel your love. Let me believe in a rebirth of joy so that I can experience now a small taste of the happiness I wish to know in eternity.

—*Dimma, an Irish monk of the seventh century*

When I feel myself tossed about in the sea of this world amidst storms and tempests, I keep my eyes fixed on you, O Mary, shining star, lest I be swallowed up by the waves.

—*Saint Bernard of Clairvaux, twelfth century*

The LORD is close to the brokenhearted,
saves those whose spirit is crushed.

—*Psalm 34:19*

THE STEADFAST

LOVE OF THE LORD

NEVER CEASES.

—LAMENTATIONS 3:22

PRAYERS FOR FAITH, HOPE, AND LOVE

I raise my eyes toward the mountains.
   From where will my help come?
My help comes from the LORD,
   the maker of heaven and earth.

God will not allow your foot to slip;
   your guardian does not sleep.
Truly, the guardian of Israel
   never slumbers nor sleeps.
The LORD is your guardian;
   the LORD is your shade
   at your right hand.
By day the sun cannot harm you,
   nor the moon by night.
The LORD will guard you from all evil,
   will always guard your life.
The LORD will guard your coming and going
   both now and forever.

—*Psalm 121*

In the weariness of this struggle, I raise my eyes to You, Lord Jesus. Let the enemy do what he will to me. I shall not fear because You are a strong defender. I have good reason to hope in You, for I shall never be confounded.

—*Saint Augustine, fourth–fifth century*

LORD, my heart is as heavy as lead, and I cannot see beyond this present state of depression. I do not ask, since it may not be your will to grant it, for immediate consolation. I ask for an increase of faith, hope, and love. Given more grace, I can endure my mood of passing gloom. I accept it in a spirit of penitence. Lord, turn my discouragement into true humility.

—*Dom Hubert van Zeller, twentieth century*

Every time a wave of discouragement tries to carry us away, we must react against it by anchoring ourselves in God by a simple movement of trust; even if our spiritual life should be reduced, for certain periods, to this exercise alone, we will not have lost anything, but we will have gained much.

—*Father Gabriel, OCD, twentieth century*

O hope, sweet sister of faith, you are that virtue which with the keys of the Blood of Christ unlock eternal life to us. You guard the city of the soul against the enemy of confusion, and when the devil tries to cast the soul into despair by pointing out the seriousness of its past sins, you do not slacken your pace, but full of energy, you persevere in fortitude, putting on the balance the price of Christ's Blood.

—*Saint Catherine of Siena, fourteenth century*

The thought of my affliction
    and my homelessness
  is wormwood and gall!
My soul continually thinks of it
    and is bowed down within me.
But this I call to mind,
    and therefore I have hope:

The steadfast love of the LORD never ceases.
    his mercies never come to an end;
they are new every morning;
    great is your faithfulness,
"The LORD is my portion," says my soul,
    "therefore I will hope in him."

    —*Lamentations 3:19–24*

When evil darkens our world, give us light.
When despair numbs our souls, give us hope.

When we stumble and fall, lift us up.
When doubts assail us, give us faith.

When nothing seems sure, give us trust.
When ideals fade, give us vision.

When we lose our way, be our guide!
That we may find serenity in Your presence,
    and purpose in doing Your will.

—*Jewish prayer*

A cheerful heart is a good medicine,
    but a downcast spirit dries up the bones.

—*Proverbs 17:22*

O Holy Spirit, give me a simple heart which will not retire within itself to savor its own sorrows, a heart magnanimous in giving itself, easily moved to compassion, a faithful, generous heart, which does not forget any favor received nor hold resentment for any injuries done to it.

—*Leonce de Grandmaison, nineteenth century*

God wants us in all things to have our contemplation and our delight in love. And it is about this knowledge that we are most blind, for some of us believe that God is almighty and may do everything, and that he is all wisdom and can do everything, but that he is all love and wishes to do everything, there we fail.

God wants to have doubtful fear, inasmuch as it induces to despair, turned in us into love by true knowledge of love.

—*Julian of Norwich, fourteenth century*

Alluding to her poems on the happiness of heaven, Saint Thérèse of the Child Jesus confesses: "When I sing . . . of the happiness of heaven and of the eternal possession of God, I feel no joy; I sing only of what *I will to believe*." This is exactly how the soul must conduct itself: *believing because it wills to believe,* not relying on what it feels or experiences, but relying solely upon the word of God. These acts of pure faith, stripped of all consolation, independent of any feeling whatsoever, are truly heroic acts. . . . The darkness of the night of the spirit has precisely this end: to accustom the soul to walk by pure faith, by heroic faith.

—*Father Gabriel, OCD, twentieth century*

I believe that God is in me as the sun is in the color and fragrance of a flower—the light in my darkness, the voice in my silence.

—*Helen Keller, twentieth century*

Blessed be the God and Father of our Lord Jesus Christ, who in his great mercy gave us a new birth to a living hope through the resurrection of Jesus Christ from the dead, to an inheritance that is imperishable, undefiled, and unfading, kept in heaven for you who by the power of God are safeguarded through faith, to a salvation that is ready to be revealed in the final time. In this you rejoice, although now for a little while you may have to suffer through various trials, so that the genuineness of your faith, more precious than gold that is perishable even though tested by fire, may prove to be for praise, glory, and honor at the revelation of Jesus Christ.

—*1 Peter 1:3–7*

Those who sow in tears
   will reap with cries of joy.
Those who go forth weeping,
   carrying sacks of seed,
Will return with cries of joy,
   carrying their bundled sheaves.

   —Psalm 126:5–6

O thou soul, most beautiful of creatures, who
so ardently longest to know the place where
thy Beloved is, that thou mayest seek Him and
be united to Him, thou art thyself that very
tabernacle where He dwells, the secret chamber
of His retreat where He is hidden.

   —Saint John of the Cross, sixteenth century

My soul, be at rest in God alone,
   from whom comes my hope.

   —Psalm 62:6

THE PEACE OF GOD

THAT SURPASSES ALL

UNDERSTANDING

WILL GUARD

YOUR HEARTS

AND MINDS

IN CHRIST JESUS.

—PHILIPPIANS 4:7

PRAYERS FOR PEACE AND HEALING

When the Creator of all things created you,
he planted in your hearts the seeds of love.
But now in you love is asleep.

The Word of God . . . sleeps in those who
are shaken by storms, but it awakes the moment
they cry out.

—Origen, third century

From the wretchedness in which I find myself
I do not ask for a spirit of hilarity. If cheerfulness
is what you want me to enjoy I accept it gladly.
All that I ask is for the strength to continue
in whatever state you wish for me. I ask to be
spared the possible evils of sadness and certainly
against self-pity, disillusion, cynicism, and
discouragement I will fight with all the energy
I can muster. Out of the depths I have cried
to you, O Lord; Lord, hear my voice.

—Dom Hubert van Zeller, twentieth century

Dear God,
I feel such pain, anxiety and depression.
I know this is not Your will for me, and yet my
   mind is held in chains by fear and paranoia.
I surrender my life, right now, to You.
Take the entire mess, all of it, now too
      complicated to
   explain to anyone but known by You
      in each detail.
Do what I cannot do.
Lift me up.
Give me a new chance.
Show me a new light.
Make me a new person.
Dear God,
This depression frightens me.
Dear God,
Please bring me peace.

—*Marianne Williamson*

There are feelings, untamed and unmanageable
        in my heart:
    The bitterness of a great hatred,
            not yet absorbed;
    The moving light of love, unrequited
            or unfulfilled,
        Casting its shafts down all the corridors
            of my days;
    The unnamed anxiety brought on
            by nothing in particular,
        Some strange forboding of coming
            disaster that does not yet appear;
    The overwhelming hunger for God that
            underscores all the ambitions, dreams
            and restlessness of my churning spirit.
Hold them, O peace of God, until Thy perfect
        work is in them fulfilled.
The Peace of God, which passeth all understanding,
        shall guard my heart and thoughts.
Into God's keeping do I yield my heart
        and thoughts,
                            yea, my life—

—*Howard Thurman, twentieth century*

To the extent that you no longer identify
yourself with your depression and that you
distinguish between your deepest, real self
and the feelings of sadness and guilt which
well up, from you know not where, then you
 have the key to healing and resurrection.

   —*Jean Vanier*

Father, I know now, if I never knew it before,
that only in Thee can my restless human heart
find any peace.

   —*Peter Marshall, twentieth century*

It is in this darkness,
when there is nothing left in us
that can please or comfort our own minds,
when we seem useless and worthy of all contempt,
when we seem to have failed,
when we seem to be destroyed and devoured . . .

It is then
that the deep secret selfishness that is too close
for us to identify is stripped away from
       our souls.
It is in this darkness that we find liberty.
It is in this abandonment that we are
       made strong.
This is the night which empties us and makes
       us pure.

   —*Thomas Merton, twentieth century*

Lift up your sick self, just as you are, and let
your desire reach out to touch the good,
gracious God, just as he is, for to touch him
is eternal health.

   —*The Cloud of Unknowing, fourteenth century*

Make me whole, O Lord, and I will become
whole! O only wise and merciful Physician,
I beseech Thy benevolence: heal the wounds
of my soul and enlighten the eyes of my mind
that I may understand my place in Thine
eternal design! And inasmuch as my heart and
mind have been disfigured, may Thy grace
repair them, for it is as true salt.

—*a Carmelite tertiary, twentieth century*

Wash away every stain,
Irrigate all dryness,
Heal every wound.

Make supple all that is rigid,
Give ardour to things grown cold,
Straighten every crooked path.

Grant to thy faithful
Who put their trust in thee,
The blessing of thy sevenfold gifts.

Grant us the reward of a virtuous life,
A death which leads to salvation,
To the gift of eternal joy.

—*Gregorian Missal*

Jesus knew that the disciples wanted to ask him,
so he said to them, "Are you discussing among
yourselves what I meant when I said, 'A little
while, and you will no longer see me, and again
a little while, and you will see me'? Very truly,
I tell you, you will weep and mourn, but the
world will rejoice; you will have pain, but your
pain will turn into joy. You have pain now;
but I will see you again, and your hearts will
rejoice, and no one will take your joy from you.

—*John 16:19–20, 22*

KEEP IN YOUR

HEART

A LOVING TRUST

IN OUR LORD.

—THE CLOUD OF UNKNOWING

PRAYERS FOR LIFE-GIVING THOUGHTS AND ACTIONS

O LORD, you have searched me and known me.
You know when I sit down and when I rise up;
  you discern my thoughts from far away.

Where can I go from your spirit?
  Or where can I flee from your presence?
If I take the wings of the morning
  and settle at the farthest limits of the sea,
even there your hand shall lead me,
  and your right hand shall hold me fast.
If I say, "Surely the darkness shall cover me,
  and the light around me become night,"
even the darkness is not dark to you;
  the night is as bright as the day,
  for darkness is as light to you.

—*Psalm 139:1–2, 7, 9–12*

O Father God,
I cannot fight this darkness by beating it with
    my hands.
Help me to take the light of Christ right into it.

—prayer from Africa

There are two kinds of sadness. The first is
begotten once anger has ceased, or from some
hurt that has been suffered or from a desire
that has been thwarted and brought to naught.
The other comes from unreasonable mental
anguish or from despair.

—John Cassian, fourth–fifth century

The memory of insults is the residue of anger.
It keeps sins alive, hates justice, ruins virtue,
poisons the heart, rots the mind, defeats
concentration, paralyses prayer, puts love at
a distance, and is a nail driven into the soul.

If anyone has appeased his anger, he has
already suppressed the memory of insults,
while as long as the mother is alive the son

persists. In order to appease the anger, love is necessary.

—*John Climacus, sixth century*

The desert tradition offers three sources for "dejection thoughts" that lead to depression. First, depression is the result of previous *anger*. Second, dejection springs from a desire for gain that has not been realized.

The third point of origin is more mysterious. Dejection seems to afflict the victim without any apparent reason. . . . Today we would call this condition chemical depression, possibly a genetic disorder. The experience is hell, and the victim is innocent.

Sorrow will always be with me. But Christ has overcome all evil, sadness, and even death itself. It is important to realize that just as I am not my thoughts, neither am I my moods and feelings. Thoughts, feelings, and moods come and go.

—*Mary Margaret Funk, OSB*

Prayers for Life-Giving Thoughts and Actions ▪ 33

A thorn was given me in the flesh, a messenger of Satan to torment me, to keep me from being too elated. Three times I appealed to the Lord about this, that it would leave me, but he said to me, "My grace is sufficient for you, for power is made perfect in weakness." So, I will boast all the more gladly of my weaknesses, so that the power of Christ may dwell in me. Therefore, I am content with weaknesses, insults, hardships, persecutions, and calamities for the sake of Christ; for whenever I am weak, then I am strong.

—*2 Corinthians 12:7b–10*

While uniting my weariness of spirit with your own agony in the garden, Lord, I unite my will with yours in surrendering to the will of the Father, I ask that this chalice may pass from me, but I ask still more that the Father's will be done.

—*Dom Hubert van Zeller, twentieth century*

Prayer is a sovereign remedy, for it lifts up the soul to God, who is our only joy and consolation.

Oppose virtuously any inclination to sadness. Although it may seem that all you do at this time is done coldly, sadly, and slugglishly, you must nevertheless persevere. . . . Sing spiritual canticles. . . .

It is also good to employ ourselves in exterior works and to vary them as much as possible. . . .

Seek the conversation of spiritual persons, and frequent their company as much as you can.

—*Saint Francis de Sales, sixteenth–seventeenth century*

Do not let yourself be dominated and crushed by these negative feelings or by your negative self-image. You need to react against them.

During this struggle, you will be helped and supported by the friend with whom you can share and by times of rest and relaxation.

—*Jean Vanier*

May Thy light shine in my thoughts; may
they be illumined by Thy rays, and may
Thy magnificent radiance gladden them,
for Thou art the sun that irradiates all.

—*Ephraim the Syrian, fourth century*

Great storms and temptations shall doubtlessly
arise during this journey, leaving you bewildered
and wondering which way to turn for help,
for your affection will feel deprived of both
your ordinary grace and your special grace.
Yet I say again: fear not. Even though you think
you have great reason to fear, do not panic.
Instead, keep in your heart a loving trust in
our Lord.

—*The Cloud of Unknowing, fourteenth century*

Jesus said to the disciples, "I tell you, ask and you will receive; seek and you will find; knock and the door will be opened to you. For everyone who asks, receives; and the one who seeks, finds; and to the one who knocks, the door will be opened."

—*Luke 11:9–10*

I offer for all those whom I have in any way grieved, vexed, oppressed, and scandalized, by word or deed, knowingly or unknowingly; that thou mayest equally forgive us all our sins, and all our offences against each other.

—*Thomas à Kempis, fourteenth century*

O Lord give me strength to refrain from the unkind silence that is born of hardness of heart; the unkind silence that clouds the serenity of understanding and is the enemy of peace.

—*from Uncommon Prayers*

You will discover how fragile and vulnerable your life, your body and your heart really are. You cannot do just anything. You have to look after yourself and treat yourself gently, enjoying relaxation, relationships, peace and prayer which will help you to stay in the light.

—*Jean Vanier*

Learn to savor how good the LORD is.

—*Psalm 34:9*

Never miss an opportunity to
study the Word of God. It settles
the mind and calms the heart.

—Rebbe Nachman of Breslov, eighteenth century

How good to celebrate our God in song;
    how sweet to give fitting praise.
The LORD rebuilds Jerusalem,
    gathers the dispersed of Israel,
Heals the brokenhearted,
    binds up their wounds,
Numbers all the stars,
    calls each of them by name.
Great is our Lord, vast in power,
    with wisdom beyond measure.

—Psalm 147:1b–5

THEY WENT OFF
IN THE BOAT
BY THEMSELVES
TO A DESERTED
PLACE.

—MARK 6:32

Prayers of Companions

Save me, God,
    for the waters have reached my neck.
I have sunk into the mire of the deep,
    where there is no foothold.

I am weary with crying out;
    my throat is parched.
My eyes have failed,
    looking for my God.

But I pray to you, LORD,
    for the time of your favor.
God, in your great kindness answer me
    with your constant help.

Rescue me from the mire;
    do not let me sink.
Do not let the floodwaters overwhelm me,
    nor the deep swallow me,
    nor the mouth of the pit close over me.
Answer me, LORD, in your generous love;
    in your great mercy turn to me.

—Psalm 69:2–3a, 4, 14–15a, 16–17

God, grant me the serenity to accept the things
I cannot change, the courage to change the
things I can, and the wisdom to know the
difference.

—*Serenity Prayer*

We do not cease praying for you and asking
that you may be filled with the knowledge
of his will through all spiritual wisdom and
understanding to live in a manner worthy
of the Lord, so as to be fully pleasing, in every
good work bearing fruit and growing in the
knowledge of God, strengthened with every
power, in accord with his glorious might,
for all endurance and patience, with joy giving
thanks to the Father, who has made you fit
to share in the inheritance of the holy ones
in light.

—*Colossians 1:9–12*

Give me grace, O God, to hearken to thy calling, and to follow thy guiding. For thou leadest us to store of all good things: thou offerest thyself and all thy goods; give us grace to receive them. Thou shewest us the way to most singular benefits; suffer us not to turn aside, until we have taken possession of them.

—*Ludovicus Vives, fifteenth century*

I cry aloud to God,
    cry to God to hear me.
On the day of my distress I seek the Lord;
    by night my hands are raised unceasingly;
    I refuse to be consoled.

I will remember the deeds of the LORD;
    yes, your wonders of old I will remember.
I will recite all your works;
    your exploits I will tell.
Your way, O God, is holy;
    what god is as great as our God?

—*Psalm 77:2–3, 12–14*

Teach me, O God, so to use all the circumstances
of my life today that they may bring forth in me
the fruits of holiness rather than the fruits of sin.
  Let me use disappointments as material
      for patience:
  Let me use success as material for thankfulness:
  Let me use suspense as material
      for perseverance:
  Let me use danger as material for courage:
  Let me use reproach as material
      for longsuffering:
  Let me use praise as material for humility:
  Let me use pleasure as material
      for temperance:
  Let me use pains as material for endurance.

—*John Baillie, twentieth century*

My spirit has become dry because it forgets
to feed on you.

—*Saint John of the Cross, sixteenth century*

The apostles gathered together with Jesus
and reported all they had done and taught.
He said to them, "Come away by yourselves
to a deserted place and rest a while." People
were coming and going in great numbers,
and they had no opportunity even to eat.
So they went off in the boat by themselves
to a deserted place.

—*Mark 6:30–32*

O Blessed Jesu Christ, who didst bid all who
carry heavy burdens to come to thee, refresh
us with thy presence and thy power. Quiet our
understandings and give ease to our hearts, by
bringing us close to things infinite and eternal.
Open to us the mind of God, that in his light
we may see light. And crown thy choice of
us to be thy servants, by making us springs
of strength and joy to all whom we serve.

—*Evelyn Underhill, twentieth century*

During supper, fully aware that the Father had put everything into his power and that he had come from God and was returning to God, [Jesus] rose from supper and took off his outer garments. He took a towel and tied it around his waist. Then he poured water into a basin and began to wash the disciples' feet and dry them with the towel around his waist.

So when he had washed their feet [and] put his garments back on and reclined at table again, he said to them, "Do you realize what I have done for you? You call me 'teacher' and 'master,' and rightly so, for indeed I am. If I, therefore, the master and teacher, have washed your feet, you ought to wash one another's feet. I have given you a model to follow, so that as I have done for you, you should also do."

—*John 13:2–5, 12–15*

If all of humanity suffers together,
the individual does not suffer.

—*African proverb*

Truly I tell you, if two of you agree on earth about anything you ask, it will be done for you by my Father in heaven. For where two or three are gathered in my name, I am there among them.

—*Matthew 18:19–20*

O blessed Lord, who hast commanded us to love one another, grant us grace that having received thine undeserved bounty, we may love everyone in thee and for thee. We implore thy clemency for all; but especially for the friends whom thy love has given to us. Love thou them, O thou fountain of love, and make them to love thee with all their heart, that they may will, and speak, and do those things only which are pleasing to thee.

—*Saint Anselm, eleventh century*

May the light of Christ, rising in glory, dispel the darkness of our hearts and minds.

—from the lighting of the Easter candle, Easter Vigil, Gregorian Missal

Blessed be the God and Father of our Lord Jesus Christ, the Father of compassion and God of all encouragement, who encourages us in our every affliction, so that we may be able to encourage those who are in any affliction with the encouragement with which we ourselves are encouraged by God. For as Christ's sufferings overflow to us, so through Christ does our encouragement also overflow.

—2 Corinthians 1:3–5

O God, before I sleep,
I remember before you all the people I love,
      and now in the silence I say their names
      to you.
All the people who are sad and lonely,
      old and forgotten,
poor and hungry and cold,
in pain of body and in distress of mind.
Bless all who specially need your blessing,
      and bless me too,
and make this a good night for me.
This I ask for your love's sake.

—*William Barclay, twentieth century*

I SHALL WALK

BEFORE THE LORD

IN THE LAND

OF THE LIVING.

—PSALM 116:9

Prayers of Gratitude for Healing

We do not lose heart. Even though our outer nature is wasting away, our inner nature is being renewed day by day.

—2 Corinthians 4:16

Paul and Barnabus strengthened the souls of the disciples and encouraged them to continue in the faith, saying, "It is through many persecutions that we must enter the kingdom of God."

—Acts 14:22

We hold as a gift more precious than gold, your love. From the beginning of creation your Son, the eternal Word, has been tossing about on the stormy waters of human souls, striving to bring peace through the gift of love. Now he has breathed over the waters of our souls, and the waves are calm. Merciful Father, we thank you.

—William of Saint Thierry, twelfth century   51

I give thanks unto God with my mind.
　I count one by one much that has come
　　to me to make me glad.
　I remember the simple delights—
　　The taste of food,
　　The tasteless refreshment of cool water,
　　The feeling of fatigue followed
　　　by restful sleep.
　　The friendly greeting of many who pass me
　　　in the daily round and whose smiles
　　　deepen my faith in ordinary kindness.
　I remember, yes, I remember,
　And in my mind I give thanks to God.
I give thanks unto God with my feelings.
　There are dangers which are now passed—
　　I escaped; how I do not know.
　Vast is my relief that my hunch was wise
　　to hold my tongue,
　　When to have spoken would have hurt far
　　　beyond my powers ever to amend or heal.
　The mood that settled was of despair
　　unrelieved and stark;
　　Then a change came out of nowhere.

All I know is
The cloud was lifted and once again
I was free.
With sheer feeling I give thanks to God.

—*Howard Thurman, twentieth century*

I thank you for the pain which reminds me of my need for you. I thank you for the peace that reassures me of your presence. I thank you for the joy I feel when I am in love and for the sorrow that calls me to seek an everlasting love. I thank you for the anger that springs from my thirst for justice and for the guilt that calls me to repentance. I thank you for hope that gives me the energy to go on and for the weariness that tells me it is time to rest. I thank you for the loneliness that calls me out of my selfishness and into the company of others and for the desire for solitude which calls me to spend time alone with you. I thank you for my feelings, dear God, I thank you for my life.

—*Mary Caswell Walsh*

I give you thanks, O LORD, with my whole heart;
   before the gods I sing your praise;
I bow down toward your holy temple
    and give thanks to your name for your
      steadfast love and your faithfulness;
    for you have exalted your name and your word
    above everything
On the day I called, you answered me,
   you increased my strength of soul.

   —Psalm 138:1–3

I am so small, a speck of dust
moving across the huge world. The world
a speck of dust in the universe.

Are you holding
the universe? You hold
onto my smallness. How do you grasp it,
how does it not
slip away?

I know so little.

You have brought me so far.

—*Denise Levertov*

I love the LORD, who listened
    to my voice in supplication,
Who turned an ear to me
    on the day I called.
I was caught by the cords of death;
    the snares of Sheol had seized me;
    I felt agony and dread.
Then I called on the name of the LORD,
    "O LORD, save my life!"

Return, my soul to your rest;
    the LORD has been good to you.
For my soul has been freed from death,
    my eyes from tears, my feet from stumbling.
I shall walk before the LORD
    in the land of the living.

—*Psalm 116:1–4, 7–9*

Acknowledgments continued from page ii.

Ah Lord, p. 1; and God, Father, p. 4: *The New Book of Christian Prayers,*
compiled by Tony Castle. New York: The Crossroad Publishing Company,
© 1986 by Tony Castle.

In me, p. 3: from *Eerdmans' Book of Famous Prayers,* comp. Veronica Zundel.
Grand Rapids, Michigan: William B. Eerdmans Publishing Company,
© 1983 Lion Publishing.

No fire, p. 6: from *The Selected Poetry of Jessica Powers*, published by ICS
Publications, Washington, D.C. All copyrights Carmelite Monastery of
Pewaukee, Wisconsin. Used with permission. (Editor's note: This poem
was written before Jessica Powers entered Carmel; written in 1939 or
1940; published in 1942.)

O Holy, p. 8; and We hold, p. 51: from *At Prayer with the Saints*, comp.
Anthony F. Chiffolo. Liguori; compilation copyright 1998 by Anthony
F. Chiffolo. Redemptorist publications can be reprinted with permission
of Liguori Publications, Liguori, Missouri 63057-9999. No other
reproduction of this material is permitted.

That prayer, p. 10: from *A Woman's Book of Faith,* ed. M. Shawn McGarry.
Secaucus, New Jersey: Carol Publishing Group. Original translation,
copyright © 1997 M. Shawn McGarry.

O God, p. 11: from *The Essential Catholic Prayer Book*. Ligouri; copyright
1999 by Judith A. Bauer. Redemptorist publications can be reprinted
with permission of Liguori Publications, Liguori, Missouri 63057-9999.
No other reproduction of this material is permitted.

When I, p. 11; In the, p. 14; Every time, p. 15; O hope, p. 15; O Holy,
p. 18; and Alluding to, p. 19: in *Divine Intimacy*, by Father Gabriel, OCD,
translated from the seventh Italian edition by the Discalced Carmelite
Nuns of Boston. New York: Desclee Company, 1966.

Lord, my, p. 14; From the, p. 23; and While uniting, p. 34: from *A Book
of Private Prayer*, by Dom Hubert van Zeller, Templegate Publishers
(templegate.com) 1960.

When evil, p. 17: from *Gates of Prayer, The New Union Prayerbook*.
New York: Central Conference of American Rabbis, copyright © 1975.

God wants, p. 18: from *Julian of Norwich, Showings*, trans. with intro. by
Edmund Colledge, OSA, and James Walsh, SJ, copyright © 1978 by
The Missionary Society of Saint Paul the Apostle in the State of New York,
Paulist Press, Incorporated, New York/Mahwah, New Jersey. Used with
permission of Paulist Press. www.paulistpress.com.

I believe, p. 19; It is, p. 26; and O God, p. 49: from *For You, O God, Prayers and Reflections*. Loyola University, Chicago, 1995. (Merton quote used with permission of the Merton Legacy Trust.)

O thou, p. 21; and Make me, p. 28: from *Carmelite Devotions and Prayers for Special Feasts of the Liturgical Year,* comp. by a Carmelite tertiary. Milwaukee: The Bruce Publishing Company, 1956. © Carmelite Monastery, Pewaukee, Wisconsin. Used with permission.

When the, p. 23; and The memory, p. 32: from *Drinking from the Hidden Fountain, A Patristic Breviary,* comp. Thomas Spidlik, trans. Paul Drake. Kalamazoo, Michigan: Cistercian Publications, 1994. © 1971 Piero Gribaudi Editore Turin, © English translation New City 1992.

Dear God, p. 24: from *Illuminata* by Marianne Williamson, copyright © 1994 by Marianne Williamson. Used by permission of Random House, Inc.

There are, p. 25; and I give, p. 52: from *Deep Is the Hunger*. Richmond, Indiana: Friends United Press, 1973.

To the, p. 26; Do not, p. 35; and You will, p. 38: from *Seeing beyond Depression* by Jean Vanier, copyright © Jean Vanier 2001, Paulist Press, Incorporated, New York/Mahwah, New Jersey. Used with permission of Paulist Press. www.paulistpress.com

Father, I, p. 26: from *The Prayers of Peter Marshall*, ed. Catherine Marshall. McGraw-Hill Book Company, Incorporated, a division of Baker Book House Company, copyright 1954 by Catherine Marshall.

Lift up, p. 27; and Great storms, p. 36: from *The Cloud of Unknowing* and *The Book of Privy Counseling*, ed. William Johnston. Garden City, New York: Image Books, a division of Doubleday & Company, Incorporated. Copyright © 1973 by William Johnston.

Wash away, p. 28: English translation of the sequence for Pentecost from *The Gregorian Missal for Sundays* notated in Gregorian chant by the monks of Solesmes. © 1990, Saint Peter's Abbey (Solesmes, Pays de Loire, France). Used with permission.

O Father, p. 32: Reprinted with permission from *A World at Prayer, the New Ecumenical Prayer Cycle,* comp. John Carden. Copyright 1990; all rights reserved. Twenty-Third Publications, Mystic, Connecticut.

There are, p. 32: from *John Cassian, Conferences,* trans. Colm Luibheid. Copyright © 1985 by Colm Luibheid, Paulist Press, Incorporated, New York/Mahwah, New Jersey. Used with permission of Paulist Press. www.paulistpress.com